Forward Tilt

By Isaac Morehouse

with Hannah Frankman

Forward

This book is about forward tilt. Forward tilt means being ready to jump on opportunities and engage. It means having drive and energy, and having momentum to back them. It's the antithesis of everything passive. People with forward tilt are the people with their eyes lit up, leaning forward, ready to take on the world.

Forward tilt is one of the most important things you can acquire to get an edge in your life journey.

This book is compiled of fifty-two short essays. Each one of these essays was originally a weekly email from Isaac Morehouse to participants going through the Praxis program. Participants and alumni get one of these emails delivered to their inbox every Monday morning.

Embarking on my career post-high school, I followed Isaac's blog and his writing for Praxis. I took the ideas and I applied them to my own life, and I used them to land jobs, start projects, and develop the forward momentum I needed to start building what I want.

The more I used these simple ideas and mindsets, the more excited I became about them - because they work.

This book doesn't just apply to businesspeople. It's directed towards the young professional, but many of its concepts are applicable to artists, creatives, anyone pursuing greatness. The thing that separates those who stagnate from those who succeed - no matter what they do - is forward tilt.

No one can give you self-actualization, because self-actualization can't be taught. But people *can* give you the tools to go out and find it, or create it.

Develop a forward tilt, and everything else will come naturally.

Strive to get better every day. Always work towards becoming the best version of yourself possible.

    - Hannah Frankman

How to Use This Book

For this book, we've whittled down nearly four years of weekly emails to a selection of just fifty-two - one for each week of the year. They've been edited and formatted to be used to direct a year-long pursuit of personal growth.

Following each essay is a page for notes. This is your place to turn the ideas offered in the essay into something concrete, tangible, and directly useful to you. We give you action items after each essay on how to use it.

But this is no formula. The goal of each weekly entry is to spark ideas and inspiration. Make it your own. Create your own weekly action items or insights. Experiment and find what works for you.

You can read through this book at any pace you like. You may want to read the whole thing once-through to familiarize yourself with the concepts, or read entries daily instead of weekly. But reading it slowly - focusing on one essay a week - will be the most valuable. Spend a whole week on each topic. Implement it. Absorb it and assimilate it. *Then* move on.

Do each essay all the way. In one year, you'll be light years beyond where you are now - and where most people who haven't read this book are.

Let's get started.

If you want more forward tilt, check out the podcast. Every Friday a 5-10 minute episode covers just one small concept. Go to discoverpraxis.com/forwardtilt to find out more and subscribe.

Part 1

"80% of success in any field is quite literally just showing up."

1. The Two Biggest Secrets to Success

There are only two things that matter in terms of opening up possibilities for success in your life:

1) What you can do that's of value to others
2) How well you can signal that value to the right people.

If you are awesome at writing, and writing is clearly valuable to many others, then you have number one down. But if no one knows or can easily discover this, you'll struggle.

If you have an amazing network of friends, a solid reputation, an excellent online presence, and lots of people know who you are and where to find you, you have number two down. But if you can't really do anything of value to others, you'll struggle.

You need the product and the signal. Better yet, *be* the product and the signal.

There is no cheat or quick fix or lottery ticket approach that will magically make you appear more valuable. You have to find out what you can do to create value, do it, and then learn how to best send your signal.

Even if you already have a job, these things are still the most important. Your company, boss, and coworkers do not exist to make you better or help you succeed. It's up to you.

Go do it.

Action Item: Note on the following page: What can you do that's of value to others? How well are you signaling that value? What can you do this week to enhance your value and your signal? Do it. Before you read next week's entry, write down what you did.

Notes:

2. Slow Down

This can never be said enough times:

You are not late.

Don't pressure yourself to accomplish X by Y time. Don't compare what you've done to the accomplishments of others at Z age. None of that matters.

Focus instead on becoming a better version of yourself every day, challenging yourself, eliminating things that make you feel dead inside, doing things that are promoting growth, and always remaining hungry and interested in the world. These are the things that matter.

Someone who busts ass, always gains more self-knowledge, and is never uninterested in learning will end up in a better place doing cooler things at a higher level than someone who panics or stresses to reach some specific goal by a certain age.

I don't care if you're sixteen or thirty-three. You are not ahead or behind, because you're not on any conveyor belt or timeline. The path you're following is your own.

Become greater one day at a time. The rest will follow.

Action Item: Write down one thing you want to do every single day this week to add value to yourself. Do it. Then write down what you did. You should have seven things written down before next week's entry.

Notes:

3. Stop Thinking About It

I've spoken with a number of people recently who have told me what they are "going to" do or "thinking about" doing.

"I'm going to email you." The email takes days or it never comes.

"I'm thinking about contacting this person to ask them if I can do X." Why ask? Just do it. If you have to ask, why haven't you already?

"I'm going to apply for this job, but I need to decide if I want to live in that city first." This makes no sense. You're not seizing an opportunity because you're analyzing an option you don't even have. You don't need to decide anything about the city until an offer is actually on the table.

If something sounds cool, interesting, or fun, take action. Contact the person. Start the project. Submit the application.

"I'm going to" and "I'm thinking about" are dangerous phrases. Keep saying them and you'll miss opportunities, delay action for weeks, and perhaps never do anything at all.

Thinking gets you nowhere. Take the leap and do the thing.

Action Item: Pick one thing you've been thinking about doing or talking about doing and do it. Start and finish it this week. Write down what you did.

Notes:

4. When You Don't Know, Work

What is your calling? Your niche? Your talent? Where do you want to focus your energy for the rest of your life?

Most of you don't know the answer to these questions at this point in your life. That's okay. But it can be frustrating to be exploring and testing and searching without knowing what that one thing is.

It's easy to slip into a limbo mindset where you keep asking questions and analyzing your situation and trying to decide where to put your energy. You'll think yourself around in circles, and you won't get anywhere, because just thinking isn't enough to answer your questions. To figure them out, you need two things: time and experience.

In the meantime, when you don't know what your calling is, just work your ass off at whatever you're doing right now. Wherever you are - job, Praxis, startup, the gym, even by yourself around your apartment - be the hardest worker. Just work hard all the time. Don't slack.

This will give you a tremendous sense of pride and confidence, and it will also speed up your discovery process. They say it takes 30-40 concentrated hours for a kid to learn to read and do basic math. Most kids spend a few hundred hours on them. Why? Because the vast majority of these hours are not concentrated or focused.

It's the same with your exploration to find your "thing." You can work your whole life and barely make progress because most of your time isn't spent doing real, hard work. If you want to progress quickly, buckle down and work in beast mode.

Everything else about you might be hereditary, but hard work is not. Have the reputation of being the hardest worker. Strive for that - not because you owe it to anyone else, but because it will make you feel awesome and help you discover your best life.

When you're lost or down or confused or in doubt or don't know what to do, create value. Work. Hard.

Action Item: Create something valuable for someone and give it to them for free. Write down what you did. It can be something at your work, for a friend, for a business you've never worked with or a perfect stranger. Write a blog post, write a customer review, create an image - just do something that creates value for someone! Document what you did.

Notes:

5. Energy vs. Stuff

I once heard a guy named Dan Sullivan say something to this effect: Your life is full of two substances, energy and stuff.

Energy is the substance that gives you life, joy, fulfillment, excitement, challenge, love, hope, sometimes pain, sometimes grief, sometimes calm, sometimes peace, but always growth and the opposite of stagnation.

Stuff is everything else. It just sort of accumulates (in some cases even physically) little by little and makes progress slower, movement more difficult, and your senses dulled. Stuff is mindless and thoughtless and easy in small doses, but it's not harmless. Every bit of stuff that gathers around you and takes up space in your existence attracts more stuff, just like mass has a gravitational pull. Pretty soon the stuff crowds out the energy and you're a big unmovable blob of humanity, with barely enough energy to lament your fate.

We all have stuff in our lives. Lots and lots of it. Like the hedges along the pond in my backyard, it must continually, perpetually be trimmed and hacked back.

Think about the activities that are life-giving. That's where your energy is. Do more of that. Always expand how much of that you do.

Think about everything else that does nothing for you but lull you into a stupor. That's the stuff. Do less of that. Always prune and decrease how much of that you do.

This sounds easy, but it's actually hard. Stuff happens when you do nothing. Energy requires action. We all know the feeling of finally going for a run after putting it off. When it's over, you think, "Man, I feel awesome. Why don't I do this more often?" Doing it made you happier than not doing it, but doing it requires effort. Sometimes it's easier to not be happy.

Don't succumb to the suffocation of stuff. Get rid of it. Sometimes clearing out the stuff involves the physical removal of things. Less useless furniture, no more books you don't even like, fewer clothes you never wear, less clutter in your car or on your desk. This can be a hugely helpful step because it symbolizes and concretizes the metaphysical presence of stuff in your life.

Kill the stuff. Feed the energy.

Action Item: On the following page, make two lists: one list of the things in your life that bring you energy, and another list for the stuff. Spend your week doing more of the things on the former list and less on the latter. Revel in the energy this brings you.

Notes:

6. Writing is More Valuable than Gold

Writing is one of the most important things you can become proficient at.

In Praxis, we expect our participants to write regularly, and to "ship" (send out into the world) what they write regularly, too. The second month in our program is devoted largely to writing. Participants blog every day, and they submit their work to third-party publications. This is an exercise both in delivering and in becoming stronger writers. The more your write, the better you get. The better you are, the better you can communicate ideas, build a network, and establish a presence.

It's time to start pushing yourself to write - and then shipping what you write - regularly. Ideally every day, or at least three times a week.

To that end, I issue a challenge: This week, either a) start a blog and get posting, and/or, b) write a letter to the editor to a local newspaper and submit it, or an article for an online magazine or outlet of your choice. If you want to really build momentum, do both.

What to write about? A few ideas come to mind:

- Write about your story. Tell us something about yourself. What defines you?
- Write about what you're learning at this point in your life. There's no better way to learn something than to write about what you read. What ideas have you found interesting lately?

- Write about the goals you've been setting for yourself, and how you intend to accomplish them.
- Write about something you've already accomplished, and how you accomplished it.
- Write about a book you just read. Write a review, or describe how it affected you.
- Write an article on a subject you're knowledgeable about.
- Write about your favorite band and why they inspire you.
- Write about this book and the challenges you've been doing.

Who's up for the challenge?

Action Item: Ship that blog post/article. Then share the link somewhere where people can actually find it.

Notes:

7. No Constraints

If you had no constraints, what would you want to be doing in nine months?

Now ask yourself what you think you'll actually be doing in nine months.

If the answers are different, why? What are the constraints? Can you identify them, name them, and list them? Can you begin to eliminate or reduce any of them?

What can you do to narrow the space between what you'd do with no constraints and what you think you'll do in reality?

I tend to think it's healthy to have goals much bigger than what seems currently possible. But don't just leave them in the realm of imagination. Always ask why they seem impossible, and what you can do to turn them into possibilities. Even if you don't get all the way there, you might be surprised how close you can come . . . and it's likely that what you thought you wanted will change in the process of thinking and moving towards it.

Try as much as possible to make the you without constraints and the you with constraints the same person.

Action Item: On the following page, write down your answers to all of the above questions. What you'd do with no constraints, what you think you'll actually be doing, and what causes the gap between them. Can you close that gap? How to get started chipping away?

We'll come back to where you want to be in nine months later, so be sure to write it down.

Notes:

8. Get Serious

I find big plans like New Year's resolutions or goals like, "I'm going to run every morning for the rest of my life" to be useful only for the first few months, if they're useful at all. I like to complete things, and I have a short attention span. This makes long-term goal-setting a bit counterproductive. If you're like me (or most humans), over time you lose momentum, and your focus and energy dies out.

Instead, try setting mini-goals, or even micro-goals. Micro-goals are to normal goals what Twitter is to a blog. For example, rather than, "I will read more this year," or "I will read two new books each month," try doing something more intense, but shorter, like, "I'll read three books I've been wanting to get to *this week*," or, "I'll read ten books in the next ten weeks". When that goal is completed, create a brand new one, totally unrelated, in some other area that you think will add to your human capital and happiness.

I find goals that last anywhere from one to twelve weeks to be ideal, and the shorter they are, the more intense they can be. I've gone as long as six months with these (a six month period in which I blogged every day, and read a book per week, and which was probably the most creative and productive time of my life), but I find that somewhere in the one- to two-month range is ideal, because I can push myself with both kinds of discipline - the urgent action of a sprint, and the sticktoitiveness of a marathon.

So, twenty weeks. What's one thing you want to do to improve yourself that will be hard, but that you can accomplish? You can do a lot in even an hour a day for twenty weeks. That's 140 hours. You could learn an instrument, read five books on a single topic (and thereby know more on that topic than 95% of the population), etc. etc.

If you genuinely want to get better at something - including success, creativity, and discipline itself - there is absolutely nothing stopping you. Pick something, create a challenge, and do it - Every. Single. Day.

Have fun with it.

Action Item: Don't read this and then let it sit. Take action! Set some micro goals. What challenge can you take on this week to improve your human capital? Write it. Do it.

Notes:

9. Just One More

Pick something you want to do today. Something you believe is good for you, something that will make you more of the kind of person you want to be. Something that isn't easy, that takes a bit of discipline.

A run.

Pushups.

Reading a book.

Studying a language.

Writing.

Whatever it is, after you do it, go one step further. Do one more. When you think you're done with your run, run for another five minutes. Do another five pushups. Finish the book.

Every time you do just one more than you thought you could, you form a belief in your brain, the belief that your will is the dominant force in your life. Nothing external has to dictate. That's a powerful habit of thought. It opens up a world of potential and possibility.

What do you want to push yourself to do today?

Action Item: Do one more.

Notes:

10. Wear the Shirt

I used to work for a company called Encore Communications, Inc. We installed telephone and internet cables for businesses, back before Wi-Fi and cell phones made hard-lines all but irrelevant.

The owner of the company mostly liked to hunt and fish, so I'd end up driving the company truck across the state, sometimes with a friend I'd hired for the day, going to businesses, installing cables, troubleshooting problems way over my head, and making up prices to charge them.

Early on I noticed something. I was only sixteen (and looked more like twelve), so showing up and asking to speak to the Controller at some car dealership was often met with weird looks. I hated waiting on other people to get started working, so asking for access to the server room and other areas was often required. The first time I did this I was nervous and unsure.

"I'm from Encore . . . Encore . . . no? No one told you we're coming? Um . . . well . . . we're installing some ethernet cables . . . sound familiar? . . . No? Is the controller here? He's out . . . well . . . okay . . . can I get into the computer room to start installing cable? Is it okay if we're in and out of the offices and drop ceilings today?"

The receptionist asked me to wait and she called a few more people. Some IT guy finally came and showed me around, with a lot more questions and skepticism.

The next time I went to a job I tried something different. I put on my polo shirt with the Encore logo, tucked it in, carried my tool pack, and quickly and confidently walked up to the receptionist, smiling but acting in a hurry and on a mission.

"I need to get into the computer room."

"Oh, sure, here's the key."

I signaled that I knew what I was doing - from my shirt to the way I walked and talked - and took charge of the situation, and she immediately and without hesitation handed a perfect stranger keys to access all the servers and phone systems for the business.

Sometimes I would be well in over my head and accidentally take down the entire inventory system, or voicemail system, or point of sale system, or PA system. I'd have no idea what I did wrong or how to fix it, but I'd confidently tell whoever came asking, "Yep, sorry for the inconvenience, should be back up shortly," like it was all part of the gig, and they'd smile and say thanks.

Then I'd frantically hit up my boss on the Nextel direct-connect (those were the days!) and ask him where I should start to figure out what broke and how to fix it.

I didn't know what I was doing. I was sent with little direction or training, and I was learning on the job. But what I learned that first day I put on the shirt and the confidence was a lesson that never left me:

No one else knows what they're doing either.

Everyone is making it up as they go. Of course ultimately I had to back up the confidence with properly installing LAN's and phone systems and fixing any problems, but there was a lot of grace and leeway - a lot more than I imagined - if I simply owned the situation and faked like I knew what I was doing all along.

It wasn't about lying, either. I found I could get away with almost anything, even an admission of ignorance, if I owned it and did not lose confidence. A customer once said, "The entire used car building's comms just went down, what happened?" and I said, "That's weird. I don't know. I think I severed the fiber-optic cable that goes under the parking lot, but I'm not really sure. I haven't worked with fiber before, but whatever it is, I'll figure it out and get it fixed." (And let me tell you, terminating hair-thin glass fibers without any scratches or cracks in a musty computer closet is a bitch!)

Remember: people want you to be confident in what you're doing more than they want you to be knowledgeable in what you're doing.

Put on the shirt, the walk, the smile, and most of all adopt an inner state of confidence even when your work requires you to make it up and learn as you go. That's what everyone else is doing too, and they have no idea what they're doing either.

Action Item: Get yourself in over your head on something this week. Say yes to something you don't yet know how to do, present yourself as more expert than you are, then figure out how to live up to it ASAP...and deliver. Commit to one thing you don't currently know how to do and do it by the end of the week.

Notes:

11. Be Selfish

Be selfish.

The word selfish has negative connotations. Most people labelled "selfish" are really just self-consumed, which is the weakest form of self-interest.

However, genuine selfishness, not pursued out of convenience (it's actually quite inconvenient) but rather as a principle can be extremely healthy. Pursuing selfishness as a principle means making decisions for yourself and in your own interest, but also desiring that others make decisions for themselves and in their own interests.

Wishing your own good as defined by you and the good of others as defined by them is a noble challenge, and it is the basis of genuine relationships and progress.

Phrases like, "Take one for the team" are typically just a way to evade genuine self-knowledge and responsibility, or to manipulate people into doing what you want rather than what they want. If you're doing something out of guilt, obligation, or sense of duty, you can always blame the collective, or you can slack, or you can remain unclear about whether you're really happy with your action. Don't give yourself that out. Know what you want to do and do it. Respect others enough to want them to do what they really want, too.

This plays out in enterprise all the time. Don't try to make a great company. Just try to make yourself great. If you are the best version of yourself and everyone else on the team is too, that's the most likely recipe for corporate success. These rules also apply to friendship, relationships, and every other form of interpersonal interaction in your life.

Action Item: Write down one area in your life where you are hiding behind "selflessness" as a way to avoid the hard work of living more happy and free. What would honest pursuit of progress look like in that area? Implement it.

Notes:

Part 2

"Here is one thing I believe with 100% certainty. And I'm right:

You are underestimating how much you are capable of."

12. Strike When the Iron's Hot

You are probably underestimating the value of the small things that you don't *have* to do, but *could* do to go above and beyond. Of these small things, timing is the simplest to master, and it probably has the most power.

When an opportunity arises, every minute that goes by before you take action reduces the amount of social capital and momentum with which you'll kick the opportunity off.

Example: you meet someone at a networking event. They mention they're trying to get a project off the ground that sounds really interesting to you. You say maybe you can help. They say, "Cool. Email me a few ideas and we'll see."

It's a Friday night and the event ends late. Totally loose, open ended, non-committal opportunity here. You want to brush up your pitch deck, look over their website, and compose an email that increases the odds you'll be able to make something work. So you take the weekend.

It's totally reasonable and acceptable to send them something Monday afternoon. There was no deadline, you're both busy, you aren't normally expected to deliver sooner.

But do you want to be normal? Acceptable? Reasonable? No worse than average?

Nothing bad will happen if, like most people, you send it Monday. But you will miss out on a *lot* of potential good. Every minute earlier you send it has a compounding effect on its value. When you seize the momentum and stand out beyond normal people, your value skyrockets.

Don't send it Monday. Send it Friday night. Always. Always be the person who is fast with everything.

Why not? There is no good excuse, except that you "can get away with it."

But this isn't school. This isn't an assignment where an 'A' is an 'A' no matter when you turn it in as long as it's by the deadline. It's the real world, where value is fluid and opportunity cost is real.

This isn't an obligation, it's an opportunity. Even if nothing comes of it. Even if you're unsure whether or not you actually want to take it on. Following up immediately will only create value for yourself and for them, and it will increase your options - not to mention the fact that you'll be able to enjoy the weekend more when there's nothing hanging over your head. If they take forever to get back to you, then you'll know something about them. The mistake won't be on you.

It's stupid to be slow. You should always be faster than anyone you know at following up and making good.

When I meet someone and they tell me they'll send me something, if it doesn't come within a day or two, I move them far down my list in terms of potential and my willingness to spend time on them. It's just reality.

Don't think in terms of deadlines and what you can get away with. Think in terms of opportunities and what you can push. Push the envelope in the other direction, asking how fast is *too* fast to respond (hint: there's no such thing. At least not at this stage in your career).

Netflix and Facebook can wait until you send those follow-ups.

Implement this. Make it your modus operandi.

Action Item: Do one thing this week that you could easily get away with doing a few weeks down the road. Beat one deadline just because you can.

Notes:

13. One Simple Question

This one is just for you. Don't share your answer with anyone.

Ask yourself this question and answer it in complete honesty, with no judgement. Then reflect on your answer. See what you can learn.

Are you in tepid pursuit of mediocrity, or relentless pursuit of greatness? Are you in pursuit of 'good enough that people will be impressed,' or 'best possible version of myself whether or not anyone notices?'

Think about it. Give yourself a 100% honest answer. No judgement. Then think about whether or not your answer is what you want it to be.

Mark my words, whichever way you answered these questions, you will find what you're pursuing. Are you going after the right thing?

Action Item: Do some honest self-examination. Fill up the adjacent notes page.

Notes:

14. There is no Timeline

Many of you know that you want to start your own business someday. Many more of you don't know it yet, but someday you'll feel this desire.

There is a tendency to get panicky if you can't see a path to your entrepreneurial dream right away. There's a tendency to panic if you can't see a path to a totally awesome, perfectly fulfilling job.

Relax. There is no timeline.

As long as you're not doing something that you truly hate - something that makes you a worse person - then you're okay. The path is long and winding. Most company founders don't start their big success until they are over 40. In fact, even in the realm of sexy, fast-paced, high-growth tech, new companies are twice as likely to be started by those 55 and up as those under 30. Yes, you heard right (check the data via the Kauffman Foundation if you're skeptical).

I used to meet with lots of millionaires (and even a few billionaires) who started with nothing and built a business from the ground up. The thing that struck me about all of their stories was how many years of experience they'd had at other jobs prior to starting a company. They often weren't intentionally preparing to go out on their own. They tended to be the best employees around, totally dominating whatever job they did until they got restless. *They never got restless before they absolutely mastered and crushed their current job.*

I think that's the best mentality. Restlessness is awesome, and it leads to innovation. But if you don't really dislike what you're doing, you rip yourself and others off by letting restlessness take over before you've mastered what you're working on. Channel that restlessness into kicking complete and total ass where you are now. It will move you closer to your entrepreneurial dreams faster than if you half-ass your work while dreaming of escape.

Stop pressuring yourself to figure it out and get there right now. The knowledge, network, experience, skills, and confidence you are building (*if* you are committed and killing it at work) are going to be your greatest aid farther down the road.

I wanted to create something like Praxis for twelve years before I had the clarity and tools needed to do it. I never would have gained those tools and that insight had I not thrown myself 100% into the jobs I had.

I am completely confident that many of you will launch your own businesses someday. It's who you are at your core that gives me this confidence, not what you're doing now, or any kind of obvious path that you're on. You'll get there.

Time is not your enemy.

Action Item: Identify one way in which you can push yourself further in your current job or activities. Write it down, and do it this week.

Notes:

15. Asking the Questions

The difference between an employee vs. an entrepreneur, leader, or "linchpin" is the mindset. The former simply learns and performs her tasks. The latter learns and performs tasks, but in the process is simultaneously and continuously asking questions *about* the task, process, customers, broader enterprise, business model, and future of the company.

The entrepreneur, leader, or "linchpin" looks at a business and immediately wants to know (and tries to calculate) costs, profit margins, weak points and advantages.

That's a mindset that must be learned.

I know you're busy grinding it out and creating value. Go a step further. Take a look at the business you're working in. If you're not working in a business, look at businesses you're familiar with.

Think long and hard about the following questions:

- What's the biggest threat to put the company out of business? (A competitor? Unhappy customer? Legal issue? Obsolescence?)
- What's the biggest constraint on growth?
- Is there a new technology or innovation that would fundamentally alter the business model?
- Who are the customers? (Not always as easy as you think. Sometimes you're not selling to the person who pays the tab).

- What do the customers think they're buying? (Peace of mind? Solving a specific problem? Happiness?)
- What do the employees think they're selling? (And is it the same as the above? e.g., you think you're selling coins, but customers think they're buying security.)
- What would happen if the CEO stopped coming to work?
- What would happen if you stopped coming to work?
- Biggest strengths/weaknesses of the business model?
- If you were to start an identical enterprise from scratch, what would it take? What would you do differently?

It might be useful for you to take these questions, add some of your own, and begin to write down your answers. It might be instructive to ask the CEO or the business's employees their thoughts on these questions.

The difference between a worker - one who gets a check to do a specific task - and a linchpin or entrepreneur is the ability to put specific tasks in the broader context of the business, industry, and economy.

Action Item: Write down the list of questions you want to know about the company you work for or another company you are interested in. See if you can find the answers yourself or by asking around.

Notes:

16. Better Late than Never

Sometimes when you commit to something (daily blogging, exercise, starting a project, learning a new skill, or writing a weekly email) you're traveling across time zones and running on no sleep and you lose track of time and day and realize at the last minute that you haven't yet delivered. You know it's too late to really ship something that's up to your full capabilities.

Those are the moments when you have the choice to inch toward extraordinary. They don't make you extraordinary, but they give you an inch. And any inch not gained is an inch lost, and you worked hard for those inches.

Ordinary says, "Crap. I failed at my goal. Oh well. I guess it was a dumb idea in the first place."

The inch that gets you just a wee bit closer to extraordinary says, "Crap. I'll fail if I don't deliver right now. Now I have to drag my ass out of bed, turn the light back on, reawaken my brain and body, and hammer out the shittiest blog post/do one push-up/finish one thing/watch one video/write one email. Grumble grumble this is shit but I did it damnit! Are you happy now?"

The quality of what you ship matters less than the act itself of shipping. Ship every day and you will become untouchable.

For every crap day, you'll have an amazing day, too. It's not a quality vs quantity tradeoff. Consistently barreling through bad days is the surest way to improve long-term quality and quantity.

Okay I wrote it. Now back to bed.

Action Item: Try this out on the small scale. What do you want to get good at? Commit yourself for a week to delivering every single day, regardless of circumstance.

Bonus: Are you doing micro-goals, like the ones we discussed earlier in the book? If you are, add this rule to your routine. There's never a good excuse to not deliver.

Notes:

17. Self Reflection

At Praxis our "why" is to help young people discover and do what makes them come alive. Our "how" is two pronged: 1) Real world experience, and 2) Self-reflection.

That second prong might seem odd. We offer apprenticeships and a coaching/curriculum experience, so the second prong might be assumed to be something like "knowledge", "learning", or, "education". But those things happen through both prongs equally.

What's unique about the self-reflection prong is that it brings something to the experience prong that separates good from great. You get good by doing. You get great by doing, doing, reflecting on how and what you do, and doing some more.

All real knowledge begins with self-knowledge. All real learning begins with learning how you learn.

The real separation between you and the crowd begins when you start learning what things make you effective. When you figure out through testing and reflecting what practices and schedules work best for you, you gain the capacity to be more efficient and deliberate in your life. The best schedules for each individual are different. Self-reflection is required to figure out what works best for the way you're wired.

Pursue those things. Come to understand how you tick. Find out what pitfalls are likely to catch you, and what methods are likely to propel you forward.

The person who knows him/herself truly and deeply will succeed farther and faster than a great talent with little self-knowledge.

Action Item: Take some time to do some introspection after you practice something in the real world. Reflect on your performance, write down what your inner experience was while you produced the outer outcome. Examine your actions as an outside observer. What can you learn?

Notes:

18. You Can't Write Wrong

How long does it take you to write a blog post?

I'm going to go out on a limb here and assume I know the answer: too long.

Since regular writing (even daily blogging, which is part of our Month 2 curriculum) is so heavily emphasized in Praxis, we hear a lot of participants and alumni talk about what happens when they try to deliver on a regular basis. The most common struggle is the amount of time it takes to write a post. Many of you have a hard time writing a post in less than an hour.

An hour a day to write isn't the worst thing in the world, but I know I wouldn't be able to write every day if I needed an hour each time.

I'm going to go out on another limb here and assume I know why it's taking so long: you don't know what to write.

Most of us don't actually type slowly. It's staring at the blank screen that takes the most time.

Everyone has different tricks to deal with this, and one of the main values of a disciplined daily writing schedule is the fact that you learn how to overcome this hurdle (and discover that you actually have a lot of great things to say!). Some common tricks are to go find some comment or article that you totally disagree with on a topic you care about. Let it fire you up and write in the moment of frustrated passion. Another trick is to glance at the books you've read, your browser history, or other things that might jog the memory of things you've recently been pondering.

Try them all. Persist until you improve.

Apart from the specific techniques, I think there's an underlying, subconscious assumption at the root of this problem: The reason it's taking you so long to write is because you think you can get it wrong.

This is the work of years of schooling, stifling your creativity and your voice. Writing assignments mess with our ability to write.

Just start writing. Hemingway's famous statement that you just need to sit down and write one true sentence, *"The truest sentence you know,"* is powerful. Just. Start. Writing.

If you have an idea in mind burning, write about that. But for all those times when you don't, don't try to come up with some big profound thing, or something that will make you look smart, or that couldn't possibly be wrong, or offensive, or misunderstood. Don't write for anyone else. Just write for you.

Write one true sentence. The truest sentence you know.

Some days, that might be something lofty, like "When I am around people all day it forces me to confront different versions of myself".

Some days it might be something totally mundane, like "I don't feel like cereal this morning."

Write the sentence that expresses total truth about your situation. Then let that guide you to the rest.

Don't worry about how it might sound to others. Fewer people read your stuff than you assume (no matter how famous you get!), and anyway, daily writing is for you, not them. Over time you'll develop a voice. You'll learn to tweak, become strategic.

For now, just get faster. There is no reason daily blogging can't be done in half an hour, or even ten minutes. Get in the habit.

Go read daily blogger Seth Godin for a week or two and you'll see what I mean. He probably spends ten minutes a day writing his posts.

Some days you'll get bit by an idea and spend an hour or more writing, but the stress of that level of intensity every day will be impractical. Don't bother chasing it.

Go write something.

Action Item: Set a timer for 15 minutes. Write everything you can think of, as fast as you can, until the timer goes off. Don't think. Just write. You can edit later, but while you're writing, don't allow yourself to worry about quality. Just produce.

Notes:

19. Not Big Enough

Here is one thing I believe with 100% certainty. And I'm right:

You are underestimating how much you are capable of.

Whatever you think you want. Whatever you see as your stretch goal. Whatever you assume would equal massive success. It's smaller than what you can accomplish.

Think bigger.

Nope, still too small. Bigger.

Nope, still thinking in terms of your present perception of "realistic."

Bigger. Bigger.

Still bigger.

There you go, now you're getting closer. Go bigger than you feel comfortable with. Go big so big that it hurts a little bit.

Then go a step bigger. There.

Live every day like that big goal is the thing you're confidently moving towards, the thing you must (and will) achieve.

I know you're capable of it. The only variable is whether or not you can accept it.

PS - I'm not bluffing, kidding, or being cute or inspirational in any way. This is factual. I know this is true of you, because I know it's also true of me.

Agere sequiter credere.

Action Item: If you threw all caution and conceptions of limitations to the wind, what would you be moving towards? Write it down. Write down everything you can think of. Get it out. Look at it. Imagine you're there. Then read this page again.

Notes:

20. The Five People: A Five Minute Exercise

By now most everyone knows the great Jim Rohn quote, "*You are the sum of the five people you spend the most time around.*" It's been used so many times it feels cliché, but it's still true.

I come back to this wisdom often in my own life. Be around good people. Be around people who are better than you at things you care about.

Here's your five minute morning exercise:

1. Make a list of the five traits you most want to gain/ enhance/improve in yourself
2. Make a list of the five people you spend the most time with.
3. Write down the one trait that most defines each person on that list.

Now compare the traits you want to add/enhance to the ones you're hanging around. How different are they? If there's great overlap, you're doubtless growing each day into a better version of yourself. If not, it might be time to deliberately build a better social/professional circle. It might take little more than going to lunch with the creative IT guy instead of the constantly critical marketing guy. It might take something dramatic like moving to a new city.

It's not about good people or bad people. It's about people that make you better, by your own goals and definitions. Not because of the raw abilities they were born with, but because of the things they choose to be.

When it comes to shaping your identity, what you do each day is less important than who you hang around with. I've become a better version of myself working on a construction crew and a startup, and a worse version working with electricians and politicians. It's not the task, it's the people.

Are you challenged and inspired by those around you? Do you respect them? Find a way to make it so.

Action Item: Don't leave this sitting. Do the above exercise. Identify ways you can shape your network to become a better version of yourself.

Notes:

21. Burden of Proof

New test for this week: Try reversing the burden of proof as much as possible and see what happens. What if instead of needing damn good reasons to do or think things, you required of yourself damn good reasons not to?

Why not start a band? Why not run a marathon? Why not write a book? Why not order a spouse through the mail from Russia? Why not....?

You won't end up doing most of these things. But in reversing the burden of proof, you'll learn a lot about yourself. Status quo bias is hugely useful and efficient. If we had to re-argue against every new thing, we'd be exhausted. But try doing it for a week, and try doing it just a little bit more in general. It's easy to assume we have reasons for not living differently than those around us, or for not following through on the ideas we have, but often we have no reasons at all.

Action Item: Do this for a week. First start with one thing. Write down one thing you've thought about doing but felt you needed a good reason. Flip the burden of proof and instead ask why you *shouldn't* do it.

Notes:

22. Your Elevator Pitch

Today's note is about your personal elevator pitch. I want you to think really long and hard on this, and I want you to come up with one of your own.

You're probably familiar with the concept of an elevator pitch for a company or project -- a fifteen-second description of the company's mission, goals, and philosophy. The format is the same for an individual. You are the most important company you'll ever work for, so it's important for you to know your mission, and the whys and hows behind your activities.

The value of the personal elevator pitch lies less in explaining yourself to others and more in the self-discovery that comes from crafting it.

A good elevator pitch contains the following characteristics:

- 15 seconds or less to say it
- Clarity
- Passion
- Swagger
- Who you are/what you do
- What's unique/novel about you
- Leave people hungry for more...you don't want it to end the conversation, but prompt exactly the kinds of questions you like answering!

For the basic structure, you can't go wrong with the world's oldest, most reliable formula of storytelling: beginning, middle and end. In this case, the beginning should be a problem statement and describe something familiar. The middle should be a surprise solution unique to you, and the end should be a tease that leaves people wanting more. Let me restate:

1. Beginning: something familiar, a pain point or problem
2. Middle: something novel, surprising, ironic, a "twist," your unique solution
3. End: something intriguing that leaves us wanting more

For the middle portion, it can be hard for us to see the most unique and valuable aspect of ourselves. Discovering it - what we do better than anyone in the world - is huge. This aspect of yourself will likely be the source of any entrepreneurial success you'll have. It's really useful to ask those who know you best what they think you do better than anyone in the world. You might be surprised. They'll likely tell you something you take for granted.

I'll give you one of my personal elevator pitches (they change sometimes) as an example:

"Lots of people aren't free because they think their dreams are dead. They're really just sleeping, and I'm here to wake them up."

I think it does a good job of hitting on the major keys. It's clear, passionate, has some swagger, conveys my motivating idea, and leaves people wanting to know what this means in more depth. It has a beginning, middle, and end.

1. Beginning: common problem most people will agree with: "lots of people aren't free/dead dreams."
2. Middle: surprise twist! The dreams are really just sleeping!

3. End: I bet you want to know how I think I'm going to wake them up.

I did not spit this out in a few minutes. It's almost embarrassing how long it took me to come up with. We're talking years. I used to describe myself as I am at the present moment: "I work for X," or "I do Y," but a good elevator pitch describes who you are in the universe. The enduring part of your being, your life, your purpose, and your journey. When I asked those close to me what I do uniquely well, they all gave me variations on, "You make people's obstacles seem easy to overcome," or "You inspire people to do more," or "You help people remember they aren't crazy for doing what they love."

Mine might be too weird or vague or cheesy for you, and as I evolve over time it may no longer work for me. I don't really use it outside of my own reflection and inner monologue anyway, so my goal isn't a good marketing line, but a good reminder to myself of who I am.

Action Item: Give it a shot. What's your elevator pitch?

Notes:

23. Dips

The honeymoon is over. You've hit the dip, the plateau, the blahs - whatever you want to call it.

This happens no matter what you're engaged in - a new job, a new relationship, a new city, a new project, or even on extended travel. You'll inevitably hit a lull after the newness and frenzy cease.

If you're going to try to live true to the advice I constantly hammer on, "don't do things you hate," and "life is too short to be bored," does this mean you should quit?

Maybe. But probably not. There may be other factors giving you hints that you should leave, but a dip by itself is not a reason to quit, nor is it an indicator that what you're doing isn't a great fit for you. It's natural. You will have a dip in anything you do, even the most fulfilling activity. Every artist, athlete, entrepreneur, or successful person will tell you that even in their most blissful activities the dip is real.

Ask yourself a series of questions when the dip comes, both to help get through it without getting depressed or desperate, and to suss out whether it's just a dip or whether it means you need a course correction:

- Did I enjoy this at some point?
- What did I enjoy about it?
- Do I value the outcome of the activity?
- Will it get me somewhere if I stick with it?

- Have any of my heroes or role models faced a dip? What if they had quit?
- Have I ever pushed through a dip before and been glad I did?
- Is there something I could change to make it better?
- Is it a problem of not being challenged enough? What challenges can I give myself?
- Is it a problem of being challenged too much? Can I ask for help?

No one but you can ultimately determine the nature of the dip and the best way to plow through it, or, if it is abundantly clear that you must, exit. Exit can mean many things, and not all of them imply quitting entirely. It may just mean some role changes, honest conversations, schedule adjustments, and anything else required to alter your situation into something that's a better fit for you.

Let me leave you with this: all the best stuff doesn't come from the inertia of newness. All the best stuff comes on the other side of the dip. Actually, much of it comes *in* the dip, but you only see it after. The dip is an opportunity to forge your character and skills. Hardship and slogging through are a crucible for refining your best traits.

If you know with your rational mind that you have good reasons for what you're doing, and the thing you're doing resonates with you, then the dip is just a dip. Get excited about who you're about to become by getting through it.

Action Item: Answer all of the questions about your current dip that were listed above. Even if you aren't currently in a dip, they're still immensely valuable sources of self-knowledge.

Look back over your life journey, too. Identify points in your life where you've been in dips. Examine them from the outside. What did you learn from them, and what came out of them? How did you cope, and how were they beneficial to you?

Notes:

Part 3

"As for New Year's resolutions, I'm a huge believer in them. I make them every morning."

24. List Checking vs. Carpe Diem

I like to get things done. I get a surge from checking items off my list and moving to the next task.

That's all well and good if I'm moving through a bunch of minor tasks and chores. But when it comes to real opportunities, simply attempting to complete things as if they're an assignment in a meaningless class is a sure way to rip myself off.

Doing the minimum acceptable is a smart strategy with stuff you don't care about (though it'd probably be smarter, if you really don't care, to not do those things at all).

If you *do* care - and be honest with yourself, because often we pretend not to care because we're lazy or afraid of doing poorly - don't just do what will get you by. Do what will give you the best opportunity imaginable to get what you want.

Don't just do work worthy of a check mark. Do work worthy of yourself.

Action Item: Write down one thing you care about that you're doing good enough, instead of your absolute best. Give it everything this week.

Notes:

25. Learning vs. Schooling

I want to take a moment to examine the value of learning vs. the process of "schooling" that most of you are familiar with.

The point of learning is to alter the patterns of your brain. It is to change the way you see and interpret the world so that you can better achieve what you want. New facts or information can alter your thinking patterns, but it's rare that raw data alone will rewire your brain, unless said data runs counter to (and therefore challenges) an accepted belief. Most learning requires a conscious examination of your paradigms and theories (which are often tacit), consumption of information in the form of new theories and facts, and a re-examination of whether your previous notions were complete or incorrect. If your answer is the latter, you then begin the work of creating new paradigms that more accurately measure up to your new level of knowledge.

This all sounds a bit esoteric, but remembering what learning actually is plays a huge part in determining how much you learn from your pursuits, and from life in general.

The schooling approach is focused much more on memorizing raw data and answering sets of predetermined questions. It doesn't ask you to rewire your brain and change your paradigms, nor does it offer you anything that might spark such changes.

You needn't understand the causal relationships in an economic order to memorize tropes like "Black Tuesday was the event that caused the Great Depression." This kind of information, which you've been loaded up with throughout your life, has very little transformative power. It doesn't get you anywhere.

The incentive structure in a schooling system encourages you to know all the answers, or worse, to be able to fake them. You have to prove that you know certain things. It doesn't care whether you've been transformed or improved by any absorbed knowledge. It doesn't care if you've learned a thing, as long as you can answer the questions, and parents and teachers can check things off their lists. You can go through all the motions but never learn at all.

Don't structure your education around memorizing facts you think people want to hear. Don't pursue memorized answers, but rather seek transformation. And never, ever hide from not knowing things, the way school teaches you to. The idea of pretending to know things you don't is antithetical to learning. Knowing you don't know something isn't something to be ashamed of, but rather, incentive to go and learn.

This isn't school. This is life. And in life, learning is not only enjoyable, but it's the difference between stagnation and growth. The world gives you a trowel, and water, and fertilizer, and seeds, and comes back later for a tour of the garden. Your growth is in your hands.

Action Item: Pick a book or article you're really interested in and read it with the explicit goal of transforming the way you think, rather than adding factual knowledge to your brain or just getting through the material. If you focus on mental transformation you may not even retain any facts during the process. That's fine. Don't feel bad about it. The point isn't to pass a test! Consciously try to focus on mental transformation.

Notes:

26. Lean Experiments or Bold Moves

There has been much talk and excitement in the last several years on the concept of the "lean startup," spurred by a book of the same name.

The idea is simple: create the smallest possible version of your idea, see how it works, identify problems and market feedback, iterate, and pivot to a new version. Rinse, repeat.

This approach has tremendous value, especially if you have modest resources, or if you know you're close to getting your idea right but aren't sure what the best way is to get the last perfect fit. It removes the pressure to get it perfect and encourages more rapid action, and it forces you to be humble and listen to what the market wants, rather than just creating what you imagine it wants.

If you aren't careful, there can be downsides. Peter Thiel takes a few swipes at the lean startup craze in his book *Zero to One*. I don't think Thiel is criticizing experimentation or the concept of shipping a product before it's in its perfect and final form, nor is he criticizing a tight budget and quick adaptations. What Thiel points out is a very real weakness of TLS mindset: its lack of clear vision.

Some startups following this trendy model have gone so far down the "iterate and pivot" path that they form a company that produces nothing in particular and serves no clear market, and instead hopes to simply run tiny tests all day long to discover what consumers want and then produce it.

This is a likely path to ruin, or best case, to producing another version of something the market already has in abundance. As Henry Ford famously stated, "If I would have asked people what they wanted, they would have said a faster horse." All the great innovations and products take imagination and vision that consumers don't yet have - which is why the thing you're building hasn't been created yet. The entrepreneur can't only ask consumers what they want. They also have to bring a new vision to the table.

The same applies to you personally. You are a company. Take from the lean startup model the idea that you needn't be perfect or complete before you start shipping. Daily blogging is a great example. Just start doing it. You can tweak the themes and style and subject matter as you go and see what's working for you. You have to enter the market in order to find where you can create value there.

But don't go too far down that path. If you are nothing more than a series of tiny tests waiting for market feedback, you'll be boring and unhappy. If you only write, for example, things that have gotten a good response before, or only "give the people what they want" based on A/B testing of what outfits to wear, you'll eventually go mad trying to decipher the good opinion of others. And you'll be less uniquely you.

Form a bold, definite vision of who you want to be. That's the core product. Then go TLS style with refining that last 10%, the non-core features and delivery mechanisms.

Action Item: Who do you want to be? What's the vision of the world you want to bring about? Write it down and keep it in the back of your mind as you do every little activity.

Notes:

27. Something Scary

Here's a challenge for today: do something scary.

Not just anything scary. Identify one goal or outcome you want, ask yourself what obstacles make it harder for you to achieve it, and then pick one thing you can do *today* to directly confront one of those obstacles.

For example, maybe one of your long-term goals is to be the leader of a company or project. Maybe one of your obstacles to attaining that goal is your shyness. What's one challenge you can take on today to attempt to chip away at that obstacle? Walk up to a stranger and ask them if you can take a picture of them and ask them a few questions for your blog.

Maybe one of your goals is to travel the world or live abroad, but one obstacle is your pickiness when it comes to food. You can't live anywhere if you can only eat Chipotle! Go find something gross and eat it today.

Action Item: 1) Identify one goal 2) list out all the obstacles between you and it and 3) devise a challenge for yourself to chip away at one obstacle before you go to bed tonight. Complete the challenge this week.

Notes:

28. The Formula for Success

This title sounds like click-bait, doesn't it?

I generally hate self-help books. I hate business books about the "three steps to greatness"" or the "five ways to win."

And yet I'm about to give you a formula for success.

This formula is not prescriptive - rather, it's descriptive. It doesn't give you anything tangible to do. It doesn't guarantee that anything will happen. It's a formula in the mathematical sense, not the chemistry sense. It's a simple understanding of concrete reality. 2+2=4, but knowing this fact does nothing for your life unless and until you have two of something and you need to make four.

The formula I'm about to give you works in a similar way. It helps you better predict, understand, and take action.

The formula for success: $(r) - (e) = S$

(r) is results, (e) is expectations, and S is success. Success is results minus expectations.

You need to have non-zero days. You need to avoid being in the negative. Anything above zero builds your reputation and social capital. Most of the time this formula is purely qualitative, and numerical values cannot be meaningfully applied. But just for fun, let's use a quantitative example.

You create the expectation with your supervisor that you will get 100 cold emails sent out today. At the end of the day you send out 100 emails. By this formula, your success value is 0, which means you're neutral. You've met your expectations. That's a surprisingly rare thing. It's a big deal. It's what an elite person does. An average person might send 90 and feel good enough, even though they'd be at -10 in our equation. You don't want to be average. You don't even want to be elite. You want to be ascendant. 150 emails would put you at +50. Now we're talking.

The tendency when discovering this formula is to focus entirely on the results end of the spectrum and get worried and stressed that you can't measure up to expectations. But remember, both (r) and (e) are variables within your control. You can set the expectations that will allow you to over-deliver and come out ahead.

But be careful. If you get into the artificial expectation lowering game, you might also lose out. Until you have an established track record with someone, expectation is the only part you can communicate up front. Set it too low and they will put you in a low category.

You want to always set expectations as high as you can reasonably deliver on, and then deliver just a little more than you thought possible. Don't get yourself in a bad situation where you sell the expectations so high you're going to be screwed. "I can get it to you tomorrow," even if fulfilled, leaves you at breakeven. Saying "I can get it to you in 48 hours," and then delivering in 24 means you're now working in the black.

Keep this formula in mind. It's simple. It's not perfect. It doesn't incorporate everything. But it's a decent truth to remember from time to time.

Be ascendant. Exceed expectations. Create success.

Action Item: Identify a time when you failed to exceed expectations. Write it down. Was it because you set the expectations too high, or because you didn't push yourself enough on the results, or both? What would have happened if you would have done either differently?

Notes:

29. It's Not That Complicated

You don't need to ask Facebook for input.

You don't need to poll anyone.

You don't need a focus group.

You don't need more skills.

You don't need to consult an expert.

You don't need to wait until you figure out steps 2-10.

You don't need a lawyer.

You don't need an accountant.

You don't need a better place to think.

You don't need more money.

You don't need to perfect it.

You don't need guarantees.

You don't need to know the outcome.

You don't need to be better than the competition.

You don't need to be better than you are.

You can become better than you are if you build it.

Just build it.

It's not that complicated.

Action Item: That thing you've been thinking about? Start it.

Notes:

30. Imitation

Imitation is the surest way to get lost on a path that is not our own, headed to a destination where we don't really want to end up. Yet we all have a strong urge to imitate others.

I'm not talking about imitating the way others do things that we want to do. Sometimes mimicking an expert can be the best place to start learning something new. I'm talking about something deeper: the phenomenon of imitating the desires of others, taking on their goals and dreams as our own.

When we avoid the very difficult work of finding what makes us come alive (often best done by simply avoiding what doesn't), we want a quick fix to give us life goals and purpose. So we ape those of the people around us.

Has it ever seemed strange that most people live in identical houses, drive identical cars at each earning phase, have identical 401k's, take identical vacations, and retire to the same identical Florida neighborhood? Do you really think human desires are so uniform? For lack of unique goals, people adopt the goals and activities they are "supposed" to desire.

Basing your desires on other people's standards makes your own success and fulfillment relative, and contingent upon the norms around you. If you grow up in one place, you'll feel like a total failure achieving the same things that could make you feel like a god in another. But why let the average of those around you dictate your fulfillment?

A lot of people avoid finding the things that really make them come alive because they're embarrassed about what they find, or afraid to go after it.

Forget all of that. It's your life. You only get one, so far as we know. Boredom is a lot worse than failure. So are your unfulfilled desires.

Forget about what everyone else does. You do you.

Action Item: Make a list of the things you desire. Go down deep, beyond the things society dictates you *should* want. What would really bring you fulfillment?

Make a second list, this one of the things you're actually pursuing. Which of these are driven by a deep, sincere desire that's entirely your own?

Notes:

31. Vocabulary

This week I want you to think about some of the things you know and do very well. Often, those are the things that are the least well-defined. A few of my favorite thinkers, Hayek and Polanyi, called this phenomenon "tacit knowledge" - the ability to do things that you can't explain to others. Sometimes you aren't even aware of these things yourself.

These things are important. They're often your greatest strengths, and the areas that will provide you with your greatest opportunities and fulfillment.

If you've heard of the Dunn-Loring Effect, it's probably been used in reference to those who are ignorant of a subject, but dramatically overestimate their knowledge of it. The less-discussed flipside of the Dunn-Loring Effect is the fact that those who are masters of something tend to dramatically underestimate their knowledge and ability.

Ideas or actions that come so easily to you that you don't even have to think about them are often things that are difficult for others. That makes your skills valuable to them.

It's not uncommon for people to assume there is no market value for their strongest skill sets, because they assume these things are easy for everyone. Yet it is almost always the case that your chance of greatest returns, economic and otherwise, will be found in doing the things that come the easiest for you. (It doesn't mean you don't work hard. The things that come easy for you, if you love them, tend to make you *want* to put in hours of practice to achieve mastery).

What does all this have to do with vocabulary?

One of the surest way to uncover the things you kick ass at and have a brilliant tacit understanding of is to give them voice. Put the concepts and practices into words. Make them explicit. Give them metaphors. Try explaining them to others.

This is one of the reasons why blogging can be so valuable for self-discovery. If I ask you to go serve an upset customer, maybe you can go do it and do it well. If I ask you to define and share the three most valuable traits needed to serve an upset customer, you will gain something additional, which is self-knowledge. The better you know your strengths, the better you can improve upon them.

When you read a book that makes you go, "Yes! That's exactly it! Someone gets it!" what you are experiencing is not an introduction to a new idea, but rather an introduction to a vocabulary for ideas you already intuitively know are true, but have never articulated. It's empowering to give them voice. It enables you to make better use of them.

In fact, a great many people have found their success merely in the act of giving vocabulary to common concepts. Long before Malcolm Gladwell, everyone knew that spending massive amounts of time on something could make you really good at it. Gladwell burned this permanently into our imaginations by coining phrases like, "10,000 hours", and "Mastery".

What powerful ideas and actions can you discover or create a vocabulary for today?

Action Item: Pick something that comes naturally to you - something so easy you don't even have to think about it.

Examine the process. Try to explain it. Write down all the vocabulary you might use that you can think of.

Notes:

32. This Relates to That

My Praxis colleague Derek Magill was talking with a guy yesterday who had (once) wanted to be a lawyer. He doesn't want to be a lawyer anymore, but he expressed that he's still trying to find career paths that have some kind of connection to law, since that had been his initial plan.

This is a dumb idea.

I'm not saying you shouldn't have interests and skills, but I am saying those interests and skills should be attached to *activities*, not *industries*.

Just because you love, say, health, doesn't mean you should only look for projects and jobs and opportunities that you can clearly connect to that field. Who knows what health will look like in a few years? Who knows what you'll be like in a few years, or what your interests will be? And who knows what things you'll learn in other industries that you can use to become an asset in the health field later?

Just do interesting stuff that's new and challenging, be around people that make you better, and don't do stuff you hate.

For some, meeting the above criteria may put you in a specific field early on. This is totally fine, but make sure it happens because you're pursuing things that interest and challenge you, not because you're trying to cram yourself into some line of work just because you think you're supposed to.

Everything builds. Accomplishment compounds. Success is success, and skills can be taken across fields and industries. Learning how to succeed is more important than what you succeed at doing. Just keep moving upwards.

There's no such thing as enjoyable, challenging work that doesn't move you closer to your dream.

Action Item: Explore job opportunities, or even just job ideas. List some. Notice which ones stand out to you as interesting because of the field. See which ones seem interesting because of the work itself. List them. Try on the idea of jobs you wouldn't normally explore because of the field they're in. When you think about the work itself, which ones excite you?

Notes:

33. Have a Clear Ask

This one is short and sweet. When you email someone or call them for professional reasons, have a clear ask.

If it's a friend or mentor and you just want to talk, no problem. But a professional contact shouldn't be contacted unless you have a clear, simple ask. Preferably just one ask, not several, and with a simple explanation, not tons of supplementary information.

Action Item: Find an email or text you wrote that included more than one ask, or a lot of fluff that wasn't necessary. Rewrite is as a simple, single ask.

Notes:

34. Secrets

There are two Biblical metaphors that I frequently recall:

"Don't throw your pearls before swine,"

and

"No one puts new wine into old wineskins, or they will burst."

Both of these statements seem a bit out of character for the man who spent his life spreading the ideas Christianity is founded upon. Both are about keeping truths from those who cannot appreciate them. A creature that doesn't know how to marvel at a pearl isn't worthy of one. A vessel that can't contain good wine shouldn't receive it.

Peter Thiel talks about the idea of secrets in his phenomenal book *Zero to One*. If you are a part of something truly powerful and world changing, what you know you're doing and what the world thinks you're doing are probably not exactly the same. You have some special inside knowledge.

This could be as simple as a business plan. McDonald's is thought of as a food business, but those in the know realize it's actually a real estate company. Their entire model revolves around this little known secret.

The word "secret" has a negative connotation. Many people associate it with maliciousness, or lies, or doublespeak, but that's not the sense in which I mean it at all. Secrets aren't only for deception or fell deeds. What I'm referring to is benign conspiracy.

I keep secrets from my kids. If they ask me what a movie is about, and it's about a serial killer who gruesomely displays his victims, I'll probably just say, "It's a scary movie about a bad guy." The details remain secret until they are ready to hear them.

Our culture has an evangelical zeal to it. The minute someone believes in an idea or a movement, or believes they have a truth of any kind, there is this notion that they ought to immediately share every detail from the rooftops, debate, blog about it, start groups, recruit. There's nothing wrong with marketing ideas and products, but only if you know exactly who your target market is and how to reach them.

It's the audience that matters. Some ideas are for you and one or two other people. Some are for a great many.

It's important, I think, to keep some of your powder dry when it comes to things that you most deeply value. Don't bare your entire soul to the entire world unless you're ready for it to be trampled underfoot.

This doesn't mean you have to be shy or duplicitous or anything of the sort. It just means you've got a little more going on behind the scenes than what meets the eye. You know the kind of people I'm talking about - the ones who, over a beer, share with you an endless stream of deep and interesting ideas and stories. Things that you couldn't find out if you followed them on Facebook alone.

So, what's the point? It's not to hide or be shy or keep a Tabula Rasa on social media. Far from it. Be seen, be known, be clear about who you are. Be findable. But always cultivate enough ideas that you've got a lot going on the back burner too.

Not everyone is ready for everything you've got!

Action Item: What's your secret mission? What are you really trying to do or be? A core part of you who are that only those closest to you have access to?

Notes:

35. Portfolio Projects

A portfolio project is a way for you to demonstrate the value you can create with a tangible product or result. It can be anything - running an event, building a website, doing a photography project, writing a business plan, creating a product, or creating a process or program for the business where you're working.

It's a way to say to the outside world not, "I'm good at X," but instead the much more powerful "I created X." Results speak volumes.

Don't just tell the world what you can do. Show them. Never underestimate the value of a portfolio project.

What projects do you have that you could turn into a portfolio? What new projects with tangible deliverables could you take on?

Big projects are good, but avoid the common pitfall of picking something too big to complete and then getting stuck in the middle. Something finished is a thousand times more valuable than something half formed.

Action Item: Write down a skill you have that you want people to know you have. Now come up with a project that will produce tangible, visible proof of this skill. Do it!

Notes:

36. Flattery is Death

Flattery can kill you in lots of ways.

Flattery will eat your time. The surest way to deviate from the things you *should* be doing and waste time and energy is to respond to flattering requests. "You're so smart and good at X, can you help me with Y?" It feels good to be in demand. But chasing the ego boost means you're losing sight of the activities that are of the highest value to you.

Don't do things just because you were flattered.

Flattery will make you weak and flabby. The most dangerous day is the one when someone says you absolutely nailed it. *"You were perfect. I'm so inspired."*

You'll want to sit in that. You'll want to repeat that success by replicating every people-pleasing detail, rather pushing yourself to grow by pursuing your principles and passion. This is dangerous. It's the perfect way to never do anything at all.

Flattery will freeze you in time. Flattery gets you looking to the past, reliving your glory, rather than moving towards the future. A little celebration is healthy. A little backward reflection for lessons is instructive. A little reconstructing of your past into your future narrative is necessary. But when flattery gets you looking back, it's not to learn or charge ahead. It's to bask. It's to get stuck.

I've met people who are puppets, easily controlled by flattery. I've met people who are puppet masters, highly skilled in finding these people and putting them to use.

It doesn't have to be sinister. Oftentimes flattery is presented with innocent intentions. But intended or not, flattery can put a premature stop to your upward trajectory.

A compliment is great. Take it. Use it. Build on it. Say thanks. Move forward.

Flattery is dangerous. Ignore it.

Action Item: Write down something you are doing because someone flattered you, instead of for internal motivations. Would you do it without the flattery? If not, stop.

Notes:

37. Relax

Just a quick word for the day: Relax.

Remember, whatever stresses and struggles you've got today and this week and next month aren't really a big deal. In the scheme of things, what you do in the immediate present isn't going to lock you in or cause you to succeed or fail. You get to create every day.

Just create today. Don't worry about the unknown. Seize the known and make the most of it - while having fun.

Action Item: Write down the thing you think matters most this week. Then think of all the reasons it doesn't matter that much in the scheme of things.

Notes:

38. Cut It

Identify one thing that makes you less happy and stop doing it for one week. Eliminate it. Cut it. Kill it.

Maybe it's staying up too late. Maybe it's reading or responding to comments on the Internet. Maybe it's taking phone calls from your Aunt Betty who you don't like talking to.

Think about it.

Action Item: Pick one thing that is making you less happy and less awesome. Stop it for a week.

Notes:

Part 4

"Life is most fully lived on the edge. Go out and stretch your comfort zone."

39. Smaller Than You Think

What if some people don't like what you do, say, build, sell, share, or pursue?

Good. If no one dislikes it, then you have one of two problems:

1. You're reaching no one.
2. You're reaching lots of people, but you aren't *really* reaching any of them.

If what you're doing pleases everyone, then it can't possibly delight anyone. If it's easy for everyone to cheer, it can't be powerful enough to change anyone's life.

You need a target market. You *only* need a target market.

If you don't have one, keep looking for one. If you do have one, focus 100% on that market and ignore everyone else.

You don't need a large target market to have a large impact. But you can't have any impact if your target market is everyone.

This goes for business, relationships, art, ideology, and everything else.

Action Item: Identify your target market. Then identify the market you're reaching. Do the two line up? Is your work strong enough for people to dislike it?

Notes:

40. Why Purpose is Killing You

If you have a sense of life purpose, it's probably caused you undue stress and confusion at times. You've probably felt like every next step and opportunity must be crammed through the filter of that purpose, and sometimes none of them seem to fit.

If you don't have a sense of life purpose, it's probably caused you undue stress and confusion at times, too. You feel like you need some mission statement to anchor your pursuits, but you just can't find one.

I want you to try something out. Free yourself from mission statements, goals, visions, or purposes that come in the form of statements. For example, don't use things like:

"I want to help people become more creative", or, "I want to achieve self-actualization", or, "I want to have the means to travel anywhere at will", or, "I want to invest in startups"

Statements like this are all well and good, but they might unnecessarily restrict you and stress you out. If you don't have some kind of statement like this, you aren't missing out as much as you might think.

Instead of statements, find questions.

Your brain engages questions at a much higher level than it does statements and facts. Answers are dead ends, while questions are frontiers. Find your questions. For example, take some of the above statements and questionize them:

"What makes people creative?", or, "What does self-actualization look like?", or, "What would happen if I was location independent?", or, "What could I do as a startup investor?"

Feel how much more fun those are?

Action Item: Try it. If you have some kind of life goal, turn it into a question. Chase it. Let the question drive you.

If you don't have a statement of life purpose, find a question instead. It doesn't have to be THE question for all of time, just a question sufficient to drive you today.

Turn goals and visions and purposes into questions. This transforms every act into philosophy, and every statement into possibility.

What would happen if you tried?

Notes:

41. Have You Changed?

Remember when you asked yourself where you'd be in nine months if you had no constraints? And where you thought you'd actually be?

You wrote down a goal: where you wanted to aim to be in nine months.

It's time to do a quick gut check. Have you made any progress? Have you missed any opportunities to make progress?

How have you changed since you did this exercise? Have your goals changed? Are you more or less confident? More or less worried? More or less excited? More or less clear on what makes you come alive?

Goals are constantly changing, and that's okay. It's natural. It's part of the discovery process. But you should always be striving to reach them.

Where were you when you did this exercise? Where are you now?

Action Item: Write down your answers to these questions. If you want to do a bonus project, write a blog post about this.

Notes:

42. Your Brain the Alchemist

Those of you who have embarked on PDP's involving daily blogging have probably learned that you have a lot more ideas floating around in your head than you imagined.

In fact, you may start to feel like you have an endless supply of things about which to write.

You feel this because it's true. Imagination is not a finite resource. In addition to this, you've spent so many years absorbing information that you have a major backlog. Once you learn how to dislodge it, the avalanche begins.

But the avalanche won't last unless you keep adding new fallen snow on top.

Imagination is not finite, but the ability to cultivate and stimulate it is.

Your brain needs food.

The wonderful thing is that these processes - idea consumption and idea creation - are mutually reinforcing. Once you've disciplined your creating, all you need to do to keep it alive (and keep doing it better) is feed more ideas into your brain. Likewise, once you learn how to consume a lot of ideas, all you need to do to utilize your creativity is start building or writing or expressing, and that stock of ideas will begin to flow.

In case you worry that reading a bunch of other people's ideas will somehow make you less able to create original ones for yourself, let me assure you that it works the other way 'round. Great songwriters listen to a lot of music. Writers read a lot. You should consume lots too.

Your brain is not a simple input-output machine. It doesn't take in a concept and then spit it out again looking mostly the same. You have a lot of weird, unique stuff floating around in there, and whatever ideas you put in will meld with all the other experiences and outlooks.

When it comes out it will have your distinctive stamp, flavor, voice.

Your brain is an alchemist.

Once you realize this you can harness it. Almost any decent input with a sufficient weight of ideas can be transformed into gold. For me, even reading children's books with my kids can provide my brain enough material for tomorrow's blog post.

So, get into the habit of creating, but never forget the constant need for consuming. Feed your brain all kinds of ideas, all the time. Every day. Then watch it do its magic.

Action Item: Pick a challenging number of pages to read or content to consume this week. Write it down. Do it.

Notes:

43. Your Most Valuable Asset

At Praxis, we talk a lot about building social capital. It's the most important thing you can accumulate. It's far more powerful than money or skills, because it indirectly opens up access to more money and skills than you could ever directly accumulate.

I'm not exaggerating when I say that I launched Praxis on $5k of credit card debt, a bunch of elbow grease, and about a million dollars worth of social capital. I had accumulated huge reserves with a large number of people. This did not happen quickly, nor by accident. No one wanted to help me because I'm just a nice, decent guy. I had very deliberately gone out of my way to be generous, send handwritten thank you notes like you wouldn't believe (I went through probably a hundred a month for years early in my career), respond to every single email, and always offer to connect people and be helpful. It paid off.

When I wanted to launch I needed legal and financial things set up, which are not my favorite. I needed design and branding work. I needed copy editing. I needed the original six curriculum modules built by people who knew more than I did. I needed a website built. I needed more things than I can even remember right now. I had no less than a dozen different people (probably more like two dozen) doing bits and pieces necessary to launch, and all for free or something very close to it. A few people got paid a little bit, a few people got small slices of equity. But for the most part, it was all cashing in of social capital.

I never planned on this major liquidation event. I just kept building social capital because I trained myself to do it and enjoy it and I knew it would be beneficial in ways I couldn't yet imagine. I didn't plan and plot exactly who to help, how much, and how it would pay off somehow. But when I had the big idea, I had access to more relational capital than almost anyone I knew. Despite not knowing what I was doing (I didn't know what "VC" stood for when I launched), I did it. With a lot of help.

Don't start cashing social capital at this point in your career. Keep building it. Don't meet someone and immediately ask them to do something inconvenient and unenjoyable (asking them for very specific advice or asking about how they succeeded are usually good ideas, because they build, rather than spend, social capital). Think of ways you could do something that makes them happier, creates value, and adds you your reputational reserve. It can be as small as a Tweet or Facebook tag like, "John Smith just gave me some excellent ideas and inspiration." People love to be praised publicly!

Make it a game. Find excuses to thank people and create value for people every day. Not just "important" people. Anyone. Your most valuable contacts will probably end up being those closest to you - business contacts, friends, young people in need of your help, etc. I used to go out of my way to interact with the (often neglected) intern pool at my last job. Some of those people ended up being more valuable to me than the company's CEO (Zak Slayback is one! He's now my Business Development Director).

Have fun. Be nice. Be helpful. Be generous.

Action Item: Send some thank-you notes. Connect some people to some other people. Go out of your way to help.

138

Notes:

44. Integrity

What is integrity?

I don't think integrity is about being "good." It's certainly not about obeying rules. It's not about pleasing other people. It's not about being liked.

Integrity is being undivided. It is being true to who you really are, what you really intend to do, and what you promise and claim. It is definiteness of purpose and singleness of mind.

A person of integrity keeps their word - not because of the value of honesty alone, but because it is not in their nature to say or promise things they do not mean and will not live up to. A person of integrity is exactly who they appear to be. A person of integrity doesn't do things, they commit to things. Once committed, they see those things through.

Living with integrity is living in line with your true self. This means you have to always be working to identify your true self, being honest about what you find, and living in accordance with it.

It's harder than it sounds to not be double-minded; of two hearts. When your significant other asks you to come to a work party, you're torn - you really don't want to go, but you don't want to leave them hanging and make them feel bad, either. The easy way out - the way that lacks integrity - is to say you'll go or not go, and then be bitter about whichever you chose. Maybe you go, and you use your willingness to endure it as passive aggressive leverage to guilt your significant other into doing something or taking pity on you. Maybe you stay, but can't enjoy the night because of the guilt. Both of these reveal a lack of internal unification.

A person of integrity might go. They might stay. Whichever they choose, they'll first discover which they truly prefer. Since doing both is not an option, they will not allow themselves to be angry at reality or play the victim. They will choose the option that they determine to be more in line with their true complex mix of desires and nature. Once chosen, they commit. They do not try to keep one foot in the other option. They do not play games, or mope, or manipulate. They may make a deal up front: "I'll go to this if you'll watch that movie with me," but they will not try to add their actions up in some invisible ledger of martyrdom. They will make their choice and stick with it, without malice, guilt, or shame. They may later decide that they would've preferred the other choice, but rather than go backwards with their emotion, they use the information for reference in making future choices.

Integrity is more important to your reputation and internal happiness than any skill or network or knowledge.

Action Item: Identify one area where who you want to be and who you are being are at war. Think through the costs, benefits, and feelings of going with one or the other. Decide, choose, and don't look back.

Notes:

45. Are You Saying Anything?

I can't stress enough the importance of clear, direct communication.

The older I get and the more successful people I interact with in the business world (not academia or nonprofits), the more I notice the to-the-point, unambiguous way in which they communicate.

If you're in a position of influence you can probably get away with some vagaries or flowery language. Yet leaders I know rarely try. Instead, young people just getting started are the ones who use far too many words to convey far too little meaning.

I'm going to share an email exchange I had with a young woman recently. She's getting a masters degree, about to finish up. I asked her what she's passionate about or what she wants to do next. This was her reply:

"I'm taking what I know from studying free market philosophies, business, entrepreneurship, and metrics and am using that to develop a framework for looking at entrepreneurial orientation, strategy, activities and inputs in orgs and linking them to financial and nonfinancial performance. I'm hoping it will add some context to measuring performance and considering operational strategy."

I read it twice and I still had no idea what it meant. I had to ask several more questions, and at one point even ask that she limit herself to one sentence when responding, because it still wasn't clear what her value proposition was.

I get it. That kind of language can get you A's in school or get you hired in some giant bureaucracy with a lot of back-patting, but it doesn't create value for anyone. It creates confusion.

If you have a choice between a simple word and a complex word, pick the simple word. Ask yourself what every sentence is supposed to convey, and then cut it so that's all it says.

After going back and forth a few times, the student I was messaging came back with something a lot more workable. "I'm passionate about helping nonprofits measure their effectiveness."

Let that be you the first time!

Action Item: Go back through some of your writing. Read it. Examine it. What can you cut? Is it clear? How can you make it more direct, clear, effective? Always say things in the simplest manner possible.

Notes:

46. Bad Advice

What's the worst piece of advice you've ever been given?

Mine came from a coworker, early on in my career. She told me to keep my head down, put in my time, be patient, focus on building my 401(k), and eventually - after a decade or more - I'd have a really cush job.

I broke every one of her suggestions.

I did not keep my head down, but rather stuck my neck out. A lot. It paid off with more interesting work every year for the first four years of my career.

I was not patient, but rather looked for the fastest way to progress - which for me meant not working towards some specified goal, but rather just eliminating stuff I hated - and was able to eliminate pretty much all elements of my jobs I didn't like within a year or two of getting them.

I built a 401(k) when it made sense, and cashed the whole thing out when it helped me launch the next venture. Money can be recreated. Time can't.

It's been a little more than a decade, and I do not have a cush job. If I did, my soul would be a shred by now. I have something much better: a real challenge that's totally unique to me and that I love more than anything but my wife and kids.

My coworker meant well. She was sharing her secrets for success. But I didn't want her version of success. I didn't know what I wanted, but I knew I wanted it on my own terms. I'd rather deviate and fail then abide and succeed in the well-defined way she embodied. Being bored is worse than failing.

There have been other bits of bad advice throughout my life. Lots of them. "Why don't you pick an easier business model, like selling online courses to universities?" was one I got when I was pitching Praxis to investors and getting 'no's. "Why don't you set it up as a post-college finishing school instead of a potential alternative so you don't piss off universities?"

The thing that all the bad advice has had in common is the fact that it's immediately rubbed me the wrong way. Good advice might be hard to hear sometimes, and it may be harder to implement. It might be scary, but it's good. In your gut you feel better having heard it, and you know that it's right. Bad advice just rubs the wrong way, makes you feel shitty and small, and you know deep down that it's wrong.

You're more right than anyone else when it comes to what makes you come alive.

This doesn't mean it's easy to access your own insight about yourself. That's the self-examination that makes for true philosophy. But if you do it, you'll find things no one else could.

Action Item: Write down one piece of advice you're really glad you ignored. What other advice should you ignore?

Notes:

47. Scarcity vs. Abundance

Scarcity is a fact of life. It is the driving force behind all of the market exchanges we engage in, the specialized skills we acquire, and the pursuit of creating wealth.

Still, there is a great paradox in the world that few are aware of. Scarcity as a physical fact will never be overcome, and it should be embraced. However, scarcity does not exist in the realm of ideas. A mindset of scarcity applied to ideas, creative power, and opportunity can destroy you.

Ideas are infinite. Human creative capacity has no limit.

Don't ever desperately cling to ideas. Don't wait for perfection before you share them with the world. Don't protect every innovative thought or creative work like it's a trade secret. It's not the scarcity or secrecy that makes an idea valuable. When you keep them to yourself until the mythical perfect moment, you develop a subconscious orientation towards ideas that sees them as rare and precious things - things to be guarded, rather than wild, adventurous things to be unleashed.

If you write every day, you'll have more to write about, not less. Put out your best work first, and even better ideas will follow. You are a font of creative capacity.

Give away ideas regularly. Business ideas, song ideas, phrases, designs, concepts - pass them all along. The more you give, the more you'll get.

When you learn to adopt a paradigm of plenty - a paradigm that doesn't fear your demise if someone else has the same idea or gets the attention you think you deserve - you will always have plenty. Plenty of ideas, plenty of friends, plenty of opportunities, plenty of adventures.

Keep creating, keep dreaming, keep doing, and keep relentlessly giving away everything you've got. Bring out the best first, give with abandon, and watch as you become creative by force of will and habit.

You'll never run out.

Action Item: Do two things this week. 1) Generate ideas. Lots of ideas. Write them down. It doesn't matter if they're good or not - just stretch your creative muscles. 2) Share ideas. Come up with ideas for other people. Bounce ideas off of people. Swap ideas. Give them away for free.

Notes:

48. Humility is Confidence

Humility isn't about pretending to know nothing. It isn't about pretending to be nothing. It isn't about being deferential to everyone. These things are false humility (which is actually a form of arrogance).

Real humility is the ability to look like a fool without feeling crushed. It's the ability to laugh at yourself when you do things that are laughable, and to learn from yourself and when you do things that are teachable.

Humility in practice looks a lot like confidence.

The humble person will confidently declare their true level of knowledge or ignorance and be unafraid to try. The prideful person will project more knowledge than they have, or hide the knowledge they have, depending on the company, and they'll be afraid to try because failure would damage their ego.

Humility means being who you are without shame or fear or regret or superiority or inferiority. It means letting yourself be seen and known as you are.

Humility means openness to be moved and awed by the universe without fear of looking uncool. When you feel a lack of confidence, consider whether it may reflect a lack of humility.

Action Item: Find some way in which you were in error or failed. Maybe you made an incorrect claim or misspelled something in a Facebook post. Don't hide it in embarrassment, but own it with laughter.

Notes:

49. I'm Just Telling Stories

I love Mondays. They're full of possibility and challenge. Something unexpected will happen, because Mondays are mysterious.

So are Tuesdays. And Wednesdays, Thursdays, Fridays, Saturdays and Sundays. I don't naturally feel this way about every day. I decided on the story I wanted to live and I told myself that story so many times every day that I began to live it. Part of this story is that every single day is ridiculously full of unknown wonders, and that it will be the most interesting, least boring day I've ever lived. Cheesy, perhaps, but it works for me.

Lest you think this is simply a "feel good" technique, let me clarify that interesting doesn't mean easy. Some days I tell myself that this will be the hardest day of my life, and that no one wants me to succeed. I internalize that story deliberately to generate a chip on my shoulder before I go to fight the demons of the day.

Here's the truth in both approaches: you are living a story in which you are both the protagonist and the author. You get to live out and create your story in real time, but ahead of time you also get to write the next chapter.

How can both of these be true? I can't answer that question. All I know is that they are. Whatever the psychological, emotional, or spiritual mechanics of it, we have the power to tell our own story to ourselves. And the stories we tell become the stories we live. As author, we can create the setting and the plot. As protagonist, we can make decisions and create within that framework.

I'm not talking about the "Imagine a red sports car and it will appear," kinds of stories. What I'm talking about is much bigger and much more important. Imagine your role in the story of the world. Imagine your character's traits and strengths and weaknesses. Imagine the kind of things that happen to and around your character. Imagine the world he or she inhabits and the people he or she interacts with. Choose the story that resonates most deeply and fills you with excitement. Tell it to yourself. Over and over again.

The best thing about your story is that it need not be constrained by practicality - or reality - to be useful and true. There's a reason why so many great coaches and leaders use metaphors about knights in armor, great battles, heroism. Most of them imagine themselves in a story like that.

Setting up a day by telling yourself a story can be great. But the real power comes when you engage in telling stories to yourself so often that living them becomes second nature.

The stories you tell yourself become your narrative. Your narrative becomes your life.

Okay. I'm off to see what crazy thing lands on my doorstep today.

Action Item: Write the outline of an epic plot you imagine yourself taking part in this week.

Notes:

50. Lesson #1: Don't Do Things You Hate

The next three weeks, starting today, are my final chances to offer you wisdom. So I'm going to pass on the three most valuable lessons I've learned in life so far, one each week.

Today's lesson is the first: Don't do things you hate.

Surprisingly, this is one of the hardest to learn. Maybe it's the Puritan ideal that suffering through drudgery purges the soul, or maybe it's the guilt, shame, fear, and obligation we allow to take on from others in the name of altruism. Whatever the cause, we are surrounded with voices, both inner and outer, that subtly nudge us into doing a lot of things that we really don't enjoy at all. If you step back and ask, "Do I actually want to be doing this?" you might be surprised at how many things get a no.

This doesn't mean don't do anything *hard*. It doesn't mean don't do anything *painful*. I ran a marathon once. The training sucked. Many times while running, I felt I would rather be sitting on the couch with a beer. But I didn't actually want that. I wanted it in a vacuum, but the real world has tradeoffs. In the world of tradeoffs, though I wanted the beer and the couch, I wanted to be able to finish a marathon *more*. I endured pain and hardship because I wanted what it would bring me.

Avoiding things you hate requires ruthless self-knowledge and self-honesty. Do I really not want to do this thing, or am I only avoiding it out of a lack of self-esteem, or lack of focus, or laziness? You can't feel embarrassed about what you discover.

As a personal example, I do not enjoy phone conversations with extended family members, or with friends I don't know very well. I used to feel bad about this preference, and subject myself to many long phone conversations that I didn't enjoy at all (and which I'm pretty sure the other party didn't enjoy either). It was a weird, guilt-based obligation. Eventually I stopped taking or returning such calls. Now I tell people I'm not much of a phone person, but shoot me an email, and let's talk when we next see each other.

Once I internalized this lesson, I made it one of my daily, weekly, and long-term goals to reduce more and more the numbers of things I do that I do not enjoy. Perhaps surprisingly, the more I focused on and succeeded at this, the more hard work I ended up doing. You might imagine pursuing this goal would result in me sitting around a lot (with beer and football), but it turns out that when you're doing things you like, you actually work well and you want to work. I became more and more productive.

Action item: Consider the biggest stressors and pain points in your life. Write them down. Stop doing them as soon as possible.

Notes:

51. Lesson #2: Do Things All the Way

This week's lesson: Do things all the way.

As long as you're not doing something you hate, you should do the shit out of whatever you're doing.

This does *not* mean only go all in for things you love. It's too hard to know what counts. What this does mean is that, as long as you don't hate it, you should do it with everything you've got. There are three primary reasons for this.

First, you'll do everything better when you do it to the best of your ability. Don't let yourself off the hook with an effort that's less than your best. Your time is too valuable to spend doing something halfway. Get results.

Second, you will be many times happier and more fulfilled if you work your ass off. Every one of us has this nagging feeling of self-doubt and unease when we're taking it easy with work, activities, and projects. When you're busting your ass, you feel pride. It's a good feeling.

Third, pouring yourself into what you're doing now is the best way to increase the likelihood of finding and succeeding in what you'll do next. Opportunities come to people who get shit done, and to those who do so with passion. Skills are acquired and networks built by those who kick ass. By pouring yourself into the now, you're creating value and doing yourself justice in the present, and you're also building the foundation for what comes next.

Action Item: Try it. For a week, do everything you do with everything you've got.

Habits create your practice. Your practice shapes who you are and everything you're going to become.

Notes:

52. Lesson #3: Be More Than What You Do

The final important lesson in my trio, and the last idea in this book: Be more than what you do.

Considering Lesson #2, it might seem odd for me to suggest you should be more than what you do. After all, doesn't "doing it all the way" mean living and breathing your work, with everything you have? Yes. Absolutely yes - so much so that I don't think you'll ever achieve #3 unless you first master #2.

Somewhat of a paradox. When you're really immersed in something, you discover things about your true self, and you gain abilities and insights that help you awaken to a fuller version of you. The feeling of being "in flow" is an experience of the self, and it exists outside of the particular activities that might have activated that state. That broader self is something you want to always stay in touch with. There are huge benefits if you do.

Being in touch with your broader self makes you better at what you do. When you can both live and breathe your work and yet not take it personally or feel despair over failures, you are unstoppable. You want the win more than anything, but when it doesn't come, you're fine, because you're more than that win. You're bigger. This mindset is a tough one to earn, but it can be done. When a mistake, or an angry customer, co-worker, or boss can ruin a day, remember - this is just something you're doing. This isn't you. If it fails, you don't fail.

A good test to see how well you're dually maintaining an all-in mentality and an "I'm more than this" mentality is the shock test. If you quit what you're doing right now and did something totally different, would your friends and family and coworkers be shocked? They should be. If they say, "What? You're doing something else? But you lived and breathed that job/business/vision/project!" that's a sign that you were in it and living it and extracting all the value out of it that you could. You did it so fully that others saw you as inseparable from it. But all along you were and are so, so much more.

Be more. Be a lot more than what you're currently working on. But never be more in a way that takes you out of the moment, or that limits your ability to be engaged. If people heard you were changing direction and said, "Yeah, she was never really into it, so I'm not surprised," then you haven't been fully engaged. (Unless, of course, the thing you're quitting is something you don't like at all, in which case you're working on #1. The better you get at #1, the less this will be the case. At some point, everything you move on from should seem like a shock because you loved it so much!).

Don't ever live life without being fully engaged. You're capable of so much more than that, and you deserve everything that being more has to offer - the depth and richness and fullness of experience that it brings.

Action Item: Write down what parts of you aren't captured by your current activities. Can you imagine being fulfilled doing something totally different than what you're currently doing? Would it surprise others if you switched?

Notes:

Afterword

Congratulations! You've reached the end of the book. Lots of people never make it that far. They start reading a book with the best of intentions, but they quit partway. Something happens -- a change of plans, a challenge at work, a minor life crisis -- or they lose momentum and become lazy.

Life is like that too. Everybody starts with the best of intentions, but most never keep pushing all the way. They stop trying. They lose their fight. They give up. Most people never reach true, deep success. Most people end up being less than they could've been.

The fact that you're reading this book at all makes you different. It means you have drive. Drive is important -- you can't be successful without it. But it isn't enough. You can't just ride on it. You have to keep working and building, always.

So what comes next? Now that you've finished the book?

Endings aren't really endings. They're beginnings. An ending is signaled by the termination of something, but really it's an opening up of a space, in which you can start something new.

You've developed some mindsets and skills that you need to be successful, and open road lays ahead. Where will you take it?

The ideas in this book are at the foundation of the Praxis philosophy, around which the entire program is built. Ideas about working hard and working smart and standing out from the crowd and developing forward tilt. You can find more ideas like these on the *Forward Tilt* podcast, on the Praxis blog, and in the Praxis program itself. If you want more, Praxis has it for you.

If you want an intensive professional boot camp, personal coaching, and a paid startup apprenticeship that ends with a full-time job offer, apply today at discoverpraxis.com/apply.

If you want weekly episodes of the *Forward Tilt* podcast, go to discoverpraxis.com/forwardtilt.

Always keep moving forward. Remember: you're capable of far more than you've ever dreamed possible.

Good luck. Have fun. Onward and upward!

About the Authors

Isaac Morehouse is the Founder and CEO of Praxis, a professional boot camp and startup apprenticeship program for those who want more than college. He is the author of seven books and hosts a weekly podcast on education, entrepreneurship, and big ideas. Isaac is dedicated to the relentless pursuit of freedom, for himself and others. He blogs regularly at isaacmorehouse.com.

Hannah Frankman is a homeschool graduate and college opt-out. A writer, teacher, and videographer, she's passionate about self-directed education, and she's taking an entrepreneurial approach to life. She works on the education team at Praxis.

When she's not busy working, you can find her practicing CrossFit, reading, playing guitar, and writing both nonfiction and fiction.

You can find more of her writing at hannahfrankman.com.

Made in the USA
Middletown, DE
10 July 2017